MUHAMMAD ALI

To Muhammad, my precious Roni, Shari, Andrew, Traci, Mel, Ali, David, Greer, Sam, Gary, Dave and Chloe: You are all the greatest—R.G.

Photo Credits: Cover, title page, p. 5, 13, 20, 45, 53, Hulton Archive/Getty Images; p. 1, 2, 3, 4, 8, 11, 14, 15, 22, 25, 27, 31, 32, 34, 37, 38, 41, 43, 44, 47, 50, Bettmann/CORBIS; p. 55, AFP/CORBIS; p. 57, Reuters NewMedia Inc./CORBIS; p. 59, Michael Brennan/CORBIS; p. 28, AP/Wide World Photos; p. 52, Michael Cooper/Allsport

Photo Research by Yvette Mangual

Library of Congress Cataloging-in-Publication Data is available.

ISBN 0-448-42812-1 (GB) A B C D E F G H I J

ISBN 0-448-42807-5 (pb) A B C D E F G H I J

MUHAMMAD ALI

by Randy Gordon
with photographs

Grosset & Dunlap • New York

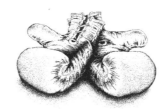

THE GREATEST

February 25, 1964—"I am the greatest! I shocked the world! I shocked the world!"

Cassius Marcellus Clay was the new heavyweight champion of the world. He had won a fight that very few people thought he could win. He had beaten Charles "Sonny" Liston. And Clay was only twenty-two years old.

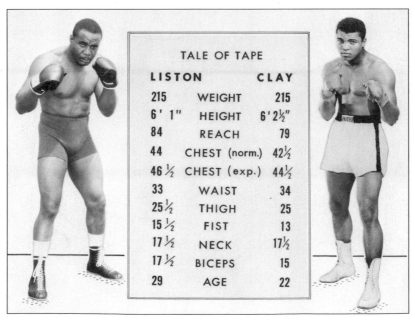

TALE OF TAPE		
LISTON		CLAY
215	WEIGHT	215
6' 1"	HEIGHT	6'2½"
84	REACH	79
44	CHEST (norm.)	42½
46½	CHEST (exp.)	44½
33	WAIST	34
25½	THIGH	25
15½	FIST	13
17½	NECK	17½
17½	BICEPS	15
29	AGE	22

Liston vs. Clay—the stats

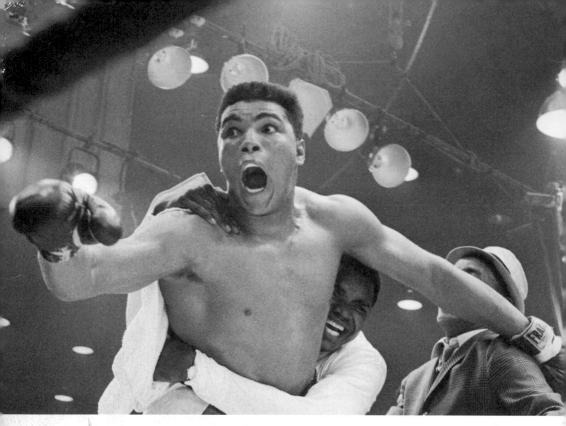

"I am the greatest!"

"I am the greatest!" Clay yelled as the ring filled with men holding TV cameras and microphones. "I am the greatest! I want everybody to bear witness—I don't have a mark on my face, and I upset Sonny Liston. I am the greatest!"

The fight took place in Miami, Florida. Liston had power. Clay had speed. Speed won.

Clay's big punch was his left jab. It was hard. It was fast—very fast.

WHAP!

Liston could not stop Clay's jab.

WHAP!

Liston's face was bleeding. His shoulder was hurt. When the bell rang to start round seven, Liston could not go on. He sat on his stool as the referee waved the fight over. Clay had become heavyweight champion of the world.

An injured Sonny Liston still puts up a fight

As the fight ended, Clay ran around the ring with his arms in the air.

"I am the greatest," he shouted. "I told all of you I would win! I am the greatest!"

The night Cassius Clay became heavyweight champion was the last time Cassius Clay ever fought. Right after the fight, he changed his religion. He became a Muslim. He also changed his name. He became Muhammad Ali.

The night Cassius Clay beat Sonny Liston was the night Muhammad Ali was born. Boxing would never be the same again.

Cassius Clay—Muhammad Ali—
at a Muslim convention

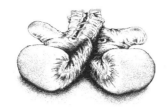

THE EARLY YEARS

Cassius Clay was born January 17, 1942, in Louisville, Kentucky. His father's name was Cassius Clay, Sr. and his mother's name was Odessa. He also had a younger brother, Rudolph Arnett Clay.

On Cassius's twelfth birthday, his parents gave him a brand-new bike. One day, Cassius rode his bike to a friend's house. When he came out, he looked around for his bike. It was gone.

Cassius Clay with his brother, Rudolph in 1963

His new bike had been stolen. Cassius was

angry. He went to the local police station to report it. The skinny twelve-year-old looked up at the policeman at the desk and said, "I want to report a stolen bike."

The policeman, Officer Joe Martin, asked Cassius to describe his bike. Cassius did. Then Cassius said to him, "If I find the kid who took my bike, I am going to beat him up. I am going to beat him real bad."

Officer Martin told Cassius that he should let the police look for the bike. Officer Martin told him that he shouldn't be thinking about bad things like beating people up.

"I don't want to beat everybody up," said Cassius. "I just want to beat up the kid who took my bike."

Officer Martin told Cassius that if he wanted to fight, he should meet him at the local gym, where he could learn to fight the right way. Cassius agreed.

At the gym, Cassius was amazed. He loved the things he saw. He saw a boxing ring. He saw punching bags. He saw lots of other kids. Some were jumping rope. Some were lifting weights. Some were wearing boxing gloves. He saw two kids in the ring. They were wearing big boxing gloves and leather helmets, called headguards.

"I want to do that," Cassius told Officer Martin.

"Do you think you are good enough?" Officer Martin asked him.

Cassius looked at him in surprise.

"Good enough?" he said. "Of course I'm good enough. I'll be the champ of this gym. Why, one day I am going to be the champion of the world."

"That's great!" said Officer Martin. "I like that spirit of yours. Let's go in."

Cassius hit the bags. He lifted weights. He jumped rope. Then he asked Officer Martin,

Twelve-year old Cassius

"When can I box?

"Not so fast, young man," Officer Martin told him. "You have to train first. You have to get in shape. You have to prove you really want to do this before you get in the ring."

"But I am in shape," Cassius told him. "And I'm fast—real fast." He threw punches at the air. He had the fastest hands Officer Martin had ever seen. Officer Martin smiled at him. He patted Cassius on the head.

"You are okay, kid. You'll be in that ring before you know it."

Officer Martin was right. Cassius was back the next day. He began showing up every day. He came right from school and wanted to stay until the gym closed.

During Cassius's first few weeks at the gym, everyone just rolled his eyes when he said he was going to be a champion one day. After a while, they all started to believe him. Cassius entered boxing tournaments. He won them with ease. He won trophy after trophy and medal after medal.

In 1959, Cassius was seventeen. The Olympics were a year away.

"I am going to be on the United States Olympic boxing team next year," he told everyone at the gym.

This time, nobody rolled his eyes.

THE GOLD MEDAL

Quickly, Clay became one of the best amateur boxers in the U.S. In 1959, Clay won the Amateur Athletic Union (AAU) light heavyweight title. This was the top amateur boxing title in the United States. He did the same thing again in 1960. That was the year the Olympics took place in Rome, Italy.

Young Clay had no trouble making the U.S. Olympic team as a light heavyweight (for fighters between 165–179 pounds).

In his first Olympic fight, Clay knocked out a tough Belgian boxer named Yan Becaus. In the quarterfinals, Clay won a 5-0 decision over a Russian fighter named Gennady Schatkov. In the semifinals, he won another 5-0 decision, this

Clay (far right) was proud to be part of the U.S. Olympic boxing team

time over an Australian named Anthony Madigan. Then, in the finals, going for the gold medal, he faced Poland's Zbigniew Pietrzykowski. Pietrzykowski was a strong and fast boxer. Many people thought he would easily defeat Clay. But the world did not know Clay yet. They did not know how great he was going to be. In the finals, they found out.

As strong as Pietrzykowski was, Clay was even stronger. As fast as Pietrzykowski was, Clay was even faster. As good a boxer as Pietrzykowski was, Clay was even better—much better. Clay danced circles around his Polish opponent. Clay landed jab after jab.

When the three-round bout ended, all five judges turned in their scorecards. Written on them were points given to the boxer the judges felt landed the most punches and stayed away from most of his opponent's punches. In amateur fights, judges award 20 points to the winner of the round and 19—or less—to the loser. All five judges decided that Clay had won each round. Cassius Clay was awarded the gold medal.

Of the ten boxers the United States sent to Rome, three won gold medals—light middleweight Wilbert McClure, middleweight Edward Crook, and light heavyweight Cassius Clay.

The United States was proud of its Olympians and medalists. Banners in downtown Louisville read WELCOME HOME TO OUR GOLD MEDALIST

CASSIUS CLAY and WELCOME TO LOUISVILLE, KENTUCKY, HOME OF OLYMPIC GOLD MEDALIST CASSIUS CLAY.

But when Clay came home, he was saddened by the things he saw. When he rode a bus in Louisville, he was made to move to the back,

The winners of Olympic medals for boxing in 1960: Cassius Clay, center, gold; Zbigniew Pietrzykowski, right, silver; and Guillio Saraudi (Italy) and Anthony Madigan (Australia), joint bronze

Ali is welcomed home by his mom after winning the gold medal

where all African-Americans were forced to ride.
One day, he and a friend went to eat in a local
restaurant. He was told that because of his
Olympic fame, he could stay. His friend, who
was African-American, was asked to leave. Clay
did not stay. He left with his friend.

That night, angry at America, Cassius threw
his gold medal into the Ohio River.

THE LOUISVILLE LIP

Only a few months after the Olympics ended, Cassius Clay left amateur boxing to become a professional. Cassius had won 134 out of 141 amateur fights, but amateur boxers do not get paid. They get medals and trophies. Pro boxers make money.

A man named Angelo Dundee trained Clay at the Fifth Street Gym in Miami, Florida. In the gym,

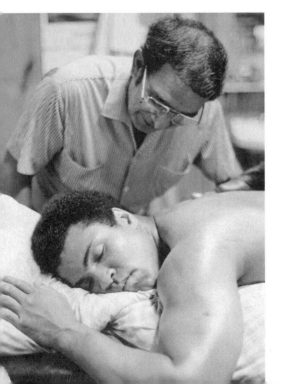

Clay loved to talk. He would tell all visitors to the gym how good he was.

One day Clay was interviewed on a radio show along with a wrestler named

Ali being worked on by his trainer, Angelo Dundee

Gorgeous George. The wrestler was bragging about himself and telling people how good he was. Clay thought the wrestler was fun to listen to. He thought that kind of bragging from a boxer would make people buy tickets. He decided to become a lot like Gorgeous George.

"I am so pretty, I should be a model, not a fighter," Clay would tell everyone. "I will be the greatest fighter of all time."

His first professional fight was on October 29, 1960. It was in Louisville against a man named Tunney Hunsaker.

The bout was six rounds. That was longer than Clay had ever fought before. All the amateur bouts Clay had fought in were scheduled for three rounds. Of course, if he knocked out or stopped an opponent, the bouts were finished in under three rounds.

A fighter is knocked out when he falls to the ground and doesn't get up before the referee counts to "ten." A fight can also be stopped when a referee refuses to let an injured boxer continue fighting. This is done for safety reasons.

Professional fighters usually begin their career by fighting in four-round and six-round bouts. As they gain experience, they move into eight-round and ten-round bouts. Championship bouts are twelve rounds. Each round is scheduled for three minutes, with a one-minute rest period between rounds.

Clay was so good that his first professional fight (against Hunsaker) was six rounds. Clay won that fight easily. Two months after beating Hunsaker, Clay knocked out Herb Siler in Miami. Before that fight, Clay had said:

"After four,
you can head for the door."

As he predicted, Siler fell in the fourth round. Clay started making up poems about each of his fights. In the poems, he would predict how the fight would go and how long it would last. "They all must fall in the round I call," he boasted.

One by one, Clay made his predictions come true.

In 1961, he won eight more fights. In 1962, he won all six of his fights by knockout. In the ring, Ali moved his feet with blinding speed. This became known as "The Ali Shuffle."

On April 19, 1961, Clay faced hard-hitting Lamar Clark, who was known as a knockout puncher. Clay had a rhyme just for Clark. It ended like this:

> *"Listen to me,*
> *what I'm sayin' is true,*
> *'ol Lamar Clark*
> *will be gone in two."*

Two rounds it was.

By this time, writers were calling Clay "The Louisville Lip." It was a nickname he loved.

As 1963 began, Clay had still not lost a professional fight. He started the year as the number two contending heavyweight. Only the ex-champion Floyd Patterson was rated higher than Clay.

Clay's first fight in 1963 was against Charlie Powell.

"Just wait and see,
Charlie Powell will fall in three."

Just as he said, Powell fell in three.

But in his second fight of 1963, against tough Doug Jones, Clay's prediction did not come true. First he said it would last six rounds. Then he said four. The fight went 10 rounds. Clay won by a decision. After the fight, he joked with writers who asked him about his wrong predictions.

"First I called it in six. Then I called it in four. Four and six, that's ten, right?"

Everyone laughed.

Clay's next fight was in London, England. The opponent was Henry Cooper. Clay's prediction was "Round Five."

"London Bridge is falling down,
So will Cooper in London Town.
I'll tell you this, it's no joke and no jive,
Henry Cooper will fall in five!"

Ali weighed in before his fight with Henry Cooper

Clay's prediction for this fight almost didn't come true. At the end of Round Four, Cooper landed a left hook on Clay's chin. Down went Clay. He pulled himself up on the ropes. Cooper got ready to charge at Clay and finish him. Then the bell rang. End of Round Four.

In Round Five, Clay landed punches on Cooper's left eyebrow, which he had cut earlier in the match. The referee stopped the fight. It was over. Clay had won.

"The Louisville Lip" was next up to challenge the current heavyweight champ, Sonny Liston, for the title.

Clay made fun of Liston. He called him the "Ugly Bear." Of course, he also made up his poetry about Liston.

"Clay swings with a left,
Clay swings with a right.
Look at young Cassius carry the fight . . .
Clay swings with a right,

At the weigh-in before the fight, Ali lunged at Liston.
Ali received a $2,500 fine.

what a beautiful swing,
and the punch raises the Bear clean out of the ring."

As he said that line, he looked up. It was as if
he was looking at Sonny leaving from the ring.

"Now Liston is still rising,
and the ref wears a frown,
for he can't start counting,
till Sonny comes down. . .

Who would have thought,
When they came to the fight,
That they'd witness the launching
Of a human satellite!"

The fight went just like his poetry said. It was easy for Clay. From the first round, Clay was way too fast for Liston. Sonny was strong, but he was no match for Clay's speed.

Cassius Clay was heavyweight champion of the world. He was just 22 years old. Ten years earlier, he had wanted to beat up someone for taking his bike. Now he had just beaten up the toughest man in the world.

ALI THE CHAMP

In November 1964, Clay was scheduled to fight
Sonny Liston again. But Clay needed a
hernia operation, so the fight was cancelled.

Six months later, the fight was rescheduled,
but Cassius Clay did not take the ring. Well,
not exactly. Cassius Clay had joined the Nation
of Islam. The Nation of Islam is a religious and
cultural community that started in the United
States in the early 1900s. When Clay joined the
Nation of Islam, Elijah Muhammad, the group's
spiritual leader, gave him a new name—
Muhammad Ali.

So on May 25, 1965, Muhammad Ali took
the ring to face Sonny Liston. The fight was held
in Lewiston, Maine, in a tiny ice skating rink in

front of the smallest crowd ever to watch a heavy-weight title fight. The fight was over quickly. Almost one minute after the bell for Round One, Liston went down from a short, quick right. The punch was so fast few people saw it. But the cameras captured it.

The punch landed on Liston's jaw. Ali had won on a first-round knockout.

Ali knocked out Liston in the first round

Six months later, Ali fought former champion Floyd Patterson. He called Patterson "The Rabbit." Ali won by a knockout in the twelfth round.

By this time, there was a war going on in Southeast Asia. It was in a small country called Vietnam. The United States sent thousands of soldiers to fight there.

American men as young as eighteen were called into the armed forces by the United States government. This was called the "draft." If you were drafted you had to go into the army. College students did not have to go. If you were weak or sick, you did not have to go. If you were a minister of any religion, you did not have to go.

Ali was not a student. He was not sick. He was not weak. Everyone knew that twenty-five-year-old Muhammad Ali would soon be called into the army. However, he said he was a Muslim minister. He had said many times that if he was drafted he would not go into the army. The world waited to see what would happen.

Ali did not wait for the draft board to call. From March 1966 to March 1967, he defended his title seven times. No heavyweight champion since has had so many title fights in one year.

In March of 1967, Ali knocked out Zora Folley. As Ali was getting ready to fight Floyd Patterson again, the draft board called him up. They wanted him to go into the U.S. Army. Of

Ali in front of Madison Square Garden

Ali at induction center

course, Ali refused to go. He said he was a
Muslim minister. He said it was against his
beliefs to belong to any army. He did not believe
in the war in Vietnam and he did not believe
what the United States was doing was right.

He was told he would be arrested if he did
not go into the Army. Ali did not care. He

believed in what he was doing, and nothing else mattered.

Ali continued to train for his next fight. Then the New York State Athletic Commission said it was taking his license and title away. The Ohio commission did the same thing. So did others. All of a sudden, Ali could not fight anywhere. He wanted to go to Europe to fight, but he was not allowed to leave the United States. He was a prisoner in his own country.

Ali lost his heavyweight title outside of the ring. He lost it without being hit by a punch.

But to many people, Ali was still the champ.

THE PEOPLE'S CHAMPION

Ali tried hard to get a license to fight. But no commission would license him. He even took his case to court. But the court took its time making a decision.

With Ali out of boxing, there was no heavyweight champion. In 1967 and 1968, two tournaments were held to find a new champion. One of the championships took place on March 4, 1968. The other title fight was held on April 27, 1968. The winner of the April 27 bout was Jimmy Ellis. Ali and Ellis knew each other from Louisville. Ellis was a good fighter, but he was no Ali.

The winner of the March fight was a hard-hitting man from Philadelphia. He had also won the Olympic heavyweight gold medal in 1964. His

name was Joe Frazier. He was called "Smokin'
Joe" because of how hard he fought.

On February 16,
1970, Joe Frazier
knocked out Jimmy
Ellis in the fifth round.
Now Frazier was the
one and only heavy-
weight champion.

Fans wanted to see
an Ali–Frazier fight.
Frazier wanted it to
happen. So did Ali.
But Ali still could not
get a license. All he
could do was talk
about the fight.

"Joe Frazier is
just holding my
title until I get back!"

Joe Frazier hugs his manager, Yank
Durham, after
defeating Jimmy Ellis

Ali said. "He is a paper champion! I am the greatest!"

As the year went on, the Vietnam War became more unpopular. During the same time, Muhammad Ali became more famous than ever. He was fun to talk to. He was on the radio. He was on TV. He was in newspapers and magazines. Everyone knew his name. Everyone knew his face.

Yes, Frazier was the champion. But Ali was "The People's Champion."

"Joe Frazier will never be the real champion until he fights me," said Ali. "I am 'The People's Champion.'"

Ali at a press conference announcing the writing of his autobiography

THE COMEBACK

The boxing world wanted Muhammad Ali to fight again. Ali wanted to fight again, too. So after three and a half years away from boxing, Ali went back into training. On October 26, 1970, he fought a tough man named Jerry Quarry. The fight took place in Georgia. Georgia did not have a boxing commission, so Ali was able to fight there.

Ali stopped Quarry in three rounds.

"I'm back and better than ever," said Ali.

Six weeks later, Ali won a court decision to fight in New York City. The fight was in New York City's Madison Square Garden against Oscar Bonavena. Ali knocked out Bonavena in Round 15. Soon after Ali beat Bonavena, "The

Fight of the Century" was announced. Everybody just called it "The Fight."

MUHAMMAD ALI vs. JOE FRAZIER.

Champion vs. Champion.

It would take place on March 8, 1971, at Madison Square Garden. Muhammad Ali's record was 31-0. Joe Frazier's record was 26-0.

The boxing world had never seen anything like it. Everybody talked about "The Fight." Of course, nobody talked more than Muhammad Ali.

"Joe is too slow to hit me!" Ali said. "I'm so

Ali and Frazier exchanged words during a contract signing ceremony

much faster than all those other guys he fought. They were slow. Joe could close his eyes and him them."

Then came some poetry:

"This may shock and amaze ya',
But I'm gonna destroy Joe Fray/zuh!"

As March 8, 1971, got closer, all anybody could talk about was "The Fight." It was one of the most exciting times the sports world had ever seen.

Muhammad Ali had won his two comeback fights. It was time for the biggest comeback fight of all.

It was time to face Joe Frazier.

THE FIGHT

March 8, 1971—This was the day New York City stopped what it was doing. On the streets and on the trains, in offices, taxis, and restaurants, all anybody could talk about was "The Fight."

"Are you going to 'The Fight?'" people asked each other.

"Will you be watching 'The Fight?'" others asked.

Every seat in Madison Square Garden was sold out. Lots of famous people were there. Some rooted for Ali. Some rooted for Frazier.

Frazier had promised to "come out smokin'." This meant he would go right after Ali as soon as the bell rang for Round One. To that, Ali said:

"Joe's gonna come out smokin',
But I ain't gonna be jokin',
I'll be pickin' and pokin'."

The two men fought as hard as they could for fifteen rounds. Sometimes, Ali would put his back on the ropes and lean on them. Then he would look out at the crowd. He would make faces and shake his head. He wanted the crowd and judges to think Frazier was not hurting him.

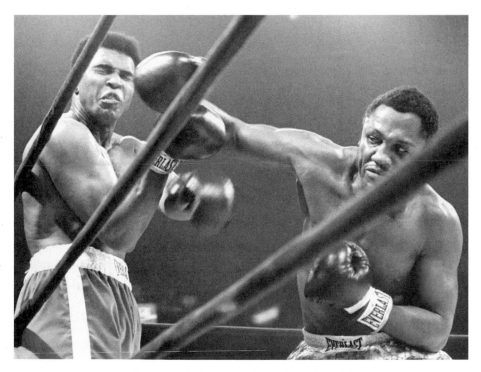

Frazier hits Ali with a hard right

Ali going down in the fifteenth round

In the fifteenth round, with just twenty-two seconds to go in the fight, Frazier threw a hard left hook. The punch landed on Ali's jaw. He went down. He landed on his back. Everyone in the crowd jumped up. Ali got up quickly. The crowd screamed and yelled. Then came the final bell. With all the noise in the building, the bell could hardly be heard.

DING-DING-DING-DING-DING!

"The Fight" was over. Frazier's face was puffy. The right side of Ali's jaw was swollen. The ring announcer read the scorecards. It was time to find out who won.

" . . . the winner, and still undefeated heavyweight champion of the world . . . ." He waited for a moment. Then he said, "Joe Frazier!"

Frazier jumped in the air. His manager hugged him. Ali lowered his head. He had lost his first fight. But for those fans who had seen "The Fight," there was no loser. Fans knew that two great fighters had just fought fifteen of the greatest rounds in boxing history.

"I will be back," Ali told his fans. "I want to fight Joe Frazier again. I will be champion again."

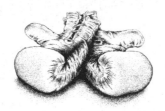

RUMBLE IN THE JUNGLE

October 30, 1974—Muhammad Ali was in the African country of Zaire, now known as the Democratic Republic of Congo. He was going to fight big George Foreman. At that time, Foreman was the heavyweight champion of the world. He had won the title on January 22, 1973, from Joe Frazier. It took George only two rounds to beat Frazier.

It was a very hot, muggy night in Zaire. In the ring, the TV lights made it feel even hotter. In Round One, Ali moved and danced away from big, strong George. But when the bell rang at the end of Round One, Ali knew he could not move and dance like that for much longer. It was just too hot.

Ali stays on the ropes as Foreman punches

In Round Two, he came out of his corner and put his back on the ropes. He kept his hands high as Foreman got close to him. Foreman punched and punched. Ali stayed on the ropes as Foreman punched. Ali hoped to make Foreman get tired. As Foreman got weaker, the large crowd yelled "Ali, *bomaye!*" ("Ali, beat him!") Later, Ali called what he was doing the "Rope-a-Dope."

Ali did the Rope-a-Dope again in Round Three. And again in Round Four. And again in Round Five. With every round, Foreman grew more tired. As he grew more tired, Ali talked to him.

"You can't hurt me, George!" said Ali. "You can't punch at all. You're not so tough!"

The more Ali talked, the harder George punched. The harder he punched, the more tired he became from the heat.

By Round Eight, Foreman was very tired. He had used all his energy in the first seven rounds. Near the end of Round Eight, Ali finally moved away from the ropes. He threw punches at Foreman. They were fast. They were hard. George spun around. Then he fell onto his back in the middle of the ring. Referee Zack Clayton began the count:

"One . . . two . . . three . . ."

Ali stood in a corner and watched.

"Four . . . five . . . six . . ."

Foreman tried to get up.

"Seven . . . eight . . ."

Foreman rolled onto his side. He tried to stand. "Nine . . . TEN!"

Clayton waved his arms. The fight was over. Muhammad Ali had done it. He had beaten George Foreman.

Muhammad Ali was once again heavyweight champion of the world.

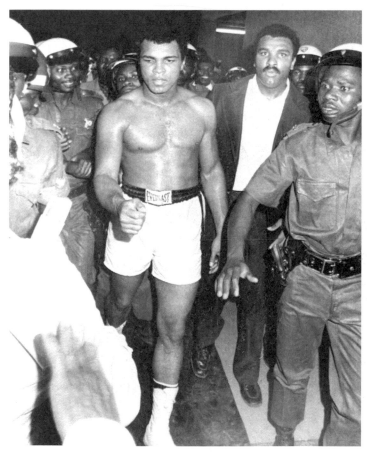

Ali walking to his dressing room after winning the Foreman fight

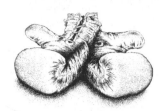

THE THRILLA IN MANILA

October 1, 1975—Ali was a busy champion in 1975. First he knocked out Chuck Wepner in March. Two months later he knocked out Ron Lyle. Two months after that, he won a decision over Joe Bugner. It was time again to face the man who had given him his two toughest fights—Joe Frazier.

Press conference where Joe Frazier agrees to fight Ali again

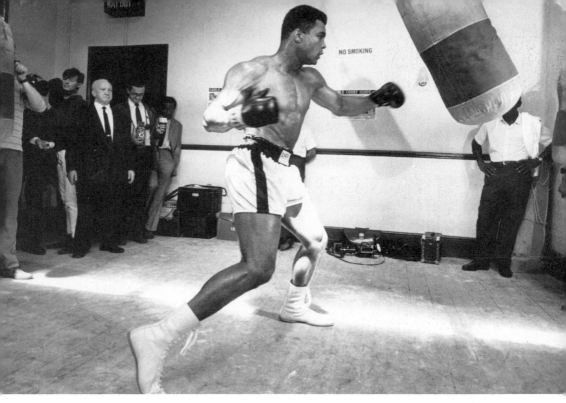

Ali trains hard for the fight

This time, the fight was held in a city named Manila in a country called the Philippines. Ali made up this poem about the fight:

"It's gonna be a chilla and a thrilla . . . in Manila."

The fight was called "The Thrilla in Manila."

Both men trained as hard as they had ever trained for a fight. They needed to be in great shape. It was over 100 degrees inside the arena. In the ring, under the hot TV lights, the temperature was closer to 130 degrees.

For round after round, the pace never slowed. When Ali danced and boxed, Frazier went right after him. When Ali used his "Rope-a-Dope," Frazier just stayed on him and banged him with hard punches. The trick that worked with Foreman in Zaire would not work here.

When Frazier stopped punching, Ali would rat-tat-tat his head with fast punches. Still, even after getting hit with a lot of punches, Frazier came right back with hard punches of his own.

By the twelfth round, the fight was even. Both men had landed a lot of punches. Both men had taken a lot of punches. In the twelfth, Ali went to work. He threw even more punches at Frazier and landed a lot of them. Frazier's nose and mouth were bleeding. His eyes were puffy. Yet he kept coming, looking to knock Ali out.

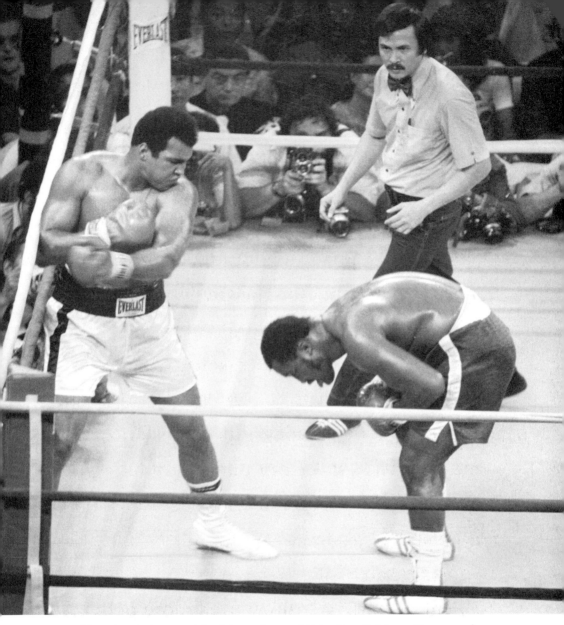

Frazier takes a big blow from Ali in the thirteenth round

In Round 13, Ali landed three hard rights. Then came a hard left-right combination to the head. Frazier was hurt. A very hard left sent

Frazier's mouthpiece flying out of the ring. Only Frazier's big championship heart kept him standing.

Ali came out for Round 14 looking for a knockout. He tore into Frazier. He threw everything he had at Joe. Jabs. Hooks. Uppercuts. Crosses. Almost everything landed. Frazier's knees wobbled.

At the bell, Frazier went back to his corner slowly. When he sat down, his trainer looked at him. He knew there was nothing left. He waved his arms. The fight was over.

Ali looked across the ring. He saw that Frazier could not continue. Then he stood up and raised his arms over his head. Ali had just won what may have been the most exciting heavyweight title fight of all time.

His greatness showed that night in "The Thrilla in Manila."

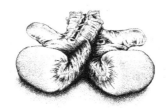

THE LATER YEARS

After "The Thrilla in Manila," Ali fought ten more times in the next six years. Four of those fights came in the year after his amazing fight against Frazier.

On February 15, 1978, the sports world was stunned. Ali was beaten in a 15-round decision. The man who beat him was 1976 Olympic light heavyweight champion Leon Spinks. Six months later, Ali became the first man to regain the heavyweight title twice when he won a 15-round decision over Spinks in a rematch.

Soon after beating Spinks, Ali retired from boxing. He was 37. For two years, Ali did not fight. During that time, a new heavyweight champion was crowned. His name was Larry

Holmes. On October 2, 1980, Ali came out of retirement to fight Holmes. He should have stayed retired. Ali didn't come out for the eleventh round, and Holmes won the fight.

One year later, Ali fought again. He faced top contender and future champion Trevor Berbick. Berbick won a ten-round decision. It was finally over. Ali retired for good. His final professional record was fifty-six wins against five losses.

By this time, Ali's speech was getting slow and

Larry Holmes defeats Ali

his hands were a bit shaky. This was probably from too many years of getting hit in the head. Doctors said he had a condition called Parkinson's syndrome. They said it would continue to get worse. They were right.

With each passing year, Ali's speech became worse and his hands trembled more. But his mind was sharp. He told people not to pity him. He visited sick people in hospitals and showed up at hundreds of dinners over the years. He traveled the world. No matter where he went—from Argentina to Asia, from Zanzibar to Zaire—people knew him. It is doubtful anybody ever signed more autographs than he did. He probably has the most famous face in history.

In 1996, Ali was honored at the start of the Games of the XXVI Olympiad in Atlanta, Georgia. Over 300 million people around the world watched as Ali, his hands shaking from Parkinson's, lit the torch to begin the Games.

Over the years, Muhammad Ali became a symbol of goodness and love, of peace and friendship. He was a champion in the ring and even more of a champion outside of it.

He really was, and still is, "The Greatest."

On July 19, 1996, Muhammad Ali receives the greatest honor— the lighting of the Olympic flame during the Opening Ceremony of the Olympic Games in Atlanta, Georgia

LADY BUTTERFLY

Cassius Clay was married one time. Muhammad Ali was married three times. Clay married Sonji Roi in 1964. When she did not adopt his Muslim faith after he won the heavyweight championship, they were divorced.

Belinda Boyd became his second wife and the mother of four of his children—daughters Maryum, twins Rasheeda and Jamilla, and son Muhammad, Jr.

Ali trains for a fight— with his daughters coming along for the ride!

Veronica Porche was his third wife and the mother of two of his daughters—Hana and Laila.

Lonnie Williams was his fourth wife. Following Ali's retirement from boxing, he and Lonnie bought a beautiful farm in Berrien Springs, Michigan. Together, Lonnie and Muhammad adopted a son, Ahad Amin.

Only one of Ali's children became a boxer—Laila.

Laila Ali was born on December 30, 1977, in Malibu, California. Laila was only three years old when her daddy retired from boxing in 1981. Her knowledge of him as a fighter comes from watching him on video tape. Her favorite fight to watch is the "Rumble in the Jungle."

When Laila was twenty-one, she told her mom and dad she was going to box. Neither one was very happy about that.

Laila Ali—ready to box

"They were not happy, but they gave me their support," said Laila. "Dad tried to talk me out of it by telling me how rough boxing can be, but he just did that to see if I really wanted to do it. I really do!"

Without any amateur fights to help her gain experience, the 5-10, 160-pound Laila fought her first professional fight on October 8, 1999. The fight took place in the small town of Verona, New York. Her opponent was April Fowler, who had lost her only other bout.

Ali knocked her out after 31 seconds of the first round. At ringside was Muhammad Ali, who blew a kiss to his daughter after the bout ended.

At the fight were hundreds of reporters with microphones and cameras. "My dad never had this much attention on him when he was first fighting," said Laila, who was called "Lady Butterfly" by the media.

After winning nine bouts without a loss, Laila faced Jacqui Frazier-Lyde, the daughter of Joe Frazier. The fight was the biggest women's boxing had ever seen. Ali danced and fought her way to winning a decision.

Muhammad Ali was not at ringside that night. He had promised to attend another function long

Laila lands a punch on Jacqui Frazier-Lyde's face

before Laila's fight date against Frazier was set. He did not want to disappoint anyone.

When news of Laila's victory was told to him he smiled. Then he asked, "She didn't get hurt, did she?" The daddy in him had come out. He smiled again when he was told neither lady was hurt.

Laila Ali began boxing because she thought it would be a good way to exercise and get in shape. She didn't realize when she first walked in the gym that soon she would become one of the best female boxers in the world.

Her footwork is a lot like her father's and so is her hand speed. So is that Ali determination, heart, and spirit. She even looks a lot like her famous dad. With all of those qualities, does that make her feel like she is "The Greatest?"

She shakes her head.

She wouldn't dare say, "I am the greatest."

She knows those words are reserved for one person—her dad.

"The greatest"